GROWING UP IN THE
FORTIES

Rebecca Hunter

HODDER
Wayland

Produced for Hodder Wayland by
Discovery Books Ltd
Unit 3, 37 Watling Street, Leintwardine, Shropshire SY7 0LW, England

First published in 2001 by Hodder Wayland, an imprint of Hodder Children's Books

British Library Cataloguing in Publication Data

Hunter, Rebecca,
    Growing up in the forties
    1. Children - Great Britain - Social life and customs -
Juvenile literature 2. Great Britain - Social life and
customs - 20th century - Juvenile literature 3. Great
Britain - Social life and customs - 1918-1945 - Juvenile
literature 4. Great Britain - Social life and customs -
1945- - Juvenile literature
    I. Title
    941 ' . 084 ' 0922

    ISBN 0 7502 3434 2

Printed and bound in Grafiasa, Porto, Portugal.

Designer: Ian Winton
Editor: Rebecca Hunter

Hodder Children's Books would like to thank the following for the loan of their material:

Art Archives: page 26 (top); Aquarius Library: page 22 (bottom); Beamish, The North of England
Open Air Museum: page 26 (bottom); Discovery Picture Library: page 14 (inset), 15 (top), 16
(inset), 19 (bottom); Hulton Getty: Cover (left), Fred Ramage, page 7 (top), 8 (bottom), 10
(bottom), 13 (top) Haywood Magee, 16 (top), 18 (top) Kurt Hutton, 18 (bottom) Bert Hardy, 22
(top) Chris Ware, 24, 28; Liverpool Museum: page 6 (top); The Leicester Mercury: page 27; The
Robert Opie Picture Collection: Cover (centre), 9 (top), 11 (top), 13 (bottom), 14 (top), 15
(bottom), 21 (both), 23, 25 (top), 30 (top).

Hodder Children's Books
A division of Hodder Headline Limited
338 Euston Road
London NW1 3BH

CONTENTS

THE 1940s

To most children, growing up in the 1940s meant growing up during the Second World War. The war started near the end of 1939 and was not over in Europe until May 1945. Everyone was affected by the war. Families were broken up as the men went away to fight. Many children also had to leave their homes when they were evacuated to the country. In this book, four people who were children during the 1940s tell us what it was like to grow up during these years.

DIANA HUNTER
Diana Hunter was born in 1935. She lived firstly in London and then in a village in Buckinghamshire.

► Diana in 1946 aged 11.

ROY WILLIAMS
Roy Williams grew up in Liverpool. He was born in 1940 and had an older brother and sister. The family spent the war years in the much-bombed city.

► Roy in 1945 aged 5.

SALLY THOMPSON

Sally Thompson was born in 1937. Her father was in the Navy and so the family moved all over the country during the forties.

▶ Sally in 1944 aged 7.

TED THOMPSON

Ted Thompson was born in 1935. He lived with his parents and younger brother in the coal-mining village of Cambois in Northumberland.

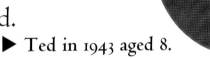

▶ Ted in 1943 aged 8.

THE WAR

In September 1939, Great Britain declared war on Germany. The war would continue for the next six years and involve many other countries all over the world.

CITY LIVING

It was dangerous living in a big city during the war. Cities were the target of enemy aircraft that flew over at night and dropped bombs. Liverpool was one of the cities that was most heavily bombed during the war. The German bombers tried to bomb the docks and hit the ships that were bringing goods and food into the country.

Roy

Our house was about a mile away from the River Mersey and the docklands, which is why many of the properties around us suffered from the bombers. Originally there were 30 houses down each side of our street. After the war there were only 15 on one side and 20 on the other!

AIR-RAIDS

Most air-raids happened at night. When an air-raid was about to happen, a siren sounded to warn people to find shelter. People found many different ways to protect themselves. Some people built Anderson shelters in their gardens. They were made of corrugated iron and were covered in turf. In London, underground stations were often used as air-raid shelters.

People building Anderson shelters in their gardens.

Sally

Young children were given all-in-one outfits called siren suits to keep them warm in air-raid shelters.

We never went to an air-raid shelter; we hid under the stairs or the kitchen table. But my suit was so warm and cosy that I often wore it outside in winter.

Forties Fact

During the war the government gave away 2.5 million Anderson shelters and 38 million gas masks.

EVACUATION

Parents were anxious that children should not remain in the dangerous cities. Many families left the cities and moved to the country.

Diana

Before the war we lived in London, not far from Battersea Power Station. My parents thought the power station would be an obvious target for enemy bombers and so we moved out of London. We went to live in a large house in Northamptonshire with several other families. This picture shows me outside the house.

Thousands of city children were evacuated by the government to the country. Families in the country were ordered to take in evacuees. Sometimes mothers went with their children, but more often the children went alone. The children were loaded onto trains with only the clothes and possessions they could carry, and their gas masks in boxes around their necks.

Forties Fact
In four days, 4,000 trains carried more than one million evacuees to the country.

During 1939 and the beginning of 1940, hardly any bombs fell and parents were tempted to bring their children home from their foster homes. The government urged parents to keep their children in the safety of the countryside.

Living in the countryside in the south of England could sometimes be as exciting as living in the cities. Many of the enemy aircraft flew over the south coast on their bombing raids.

Sally

In the summer of 1943 we were living in Sussex. We used to have picnics on the Downs.

I once remember watching a dog fight between a German plane and one of ours. It ended with the German plane crashing in the sea with much smoke and flames. It was very exciting but rather frightening too.

WORK

The 1930s had been a time of high unemployment but the war brought many more jobs for everyone. Millions of men went to fight, leaving jobs vacant at home. Some men did not join up because they had important jobs to do at home, such as farming or mining, or making aircraft or ships' engines.

Ted

I grew up in a colliery village. My granddad, father and uncle worked in the mines. Coal was much needed during the war so miners didn't have to join the forces. Towards the end of the war extra miners had to be drafted in to work. This picture shows some of the miners having a tea break down the pit.

Men who were too old for the armed forces, joined the Home Guard. This organization was intended to help defend Britain against the German invasion.

The Home Guard during training.

THEN & NOW

- The average weekly wage for a man in 1945 was £3 18s (£3.90). Now it is nearly £400.

WOMEN AT WORK

Many women took over the work men usually did: in factories or driving buses and ambulances. Other women joined special branches of the armed services.

The Women's Land Army was started to provide women to work on farms producing the food the country needed. It was difficult to attract enough volunteers and the government mounted a big advertising campaign.

For a healthy, happy job

Join the
WOMEN'S
LAND
ARMY

for details — CLIVE UPTON —
APPLY TO NEAREST W.L.A COUNTY OFFICE OR TO W.L.A HEADQUARTERS 6 CHESHAM PLACE LONDON S.W.1 STREET

FARMING

Producing enough food to feed the country during the war was a very important job. Some men who were too old or young to fight stayed at home and worked on the farms.

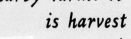

Sally

This picture shows my mother visiting the men on the nearby farm. It is harvest time and the machine is a 'thrasher' which separated the wheat from the straw. The straw was built up into huge stacks which my friends and I enjoyed playing on!

HOME LIFE

HOUSES

Houses in the forties had few of the things that we now consider essential. Some had no indoor toilets, and central heating was still a thing of the future for most people.

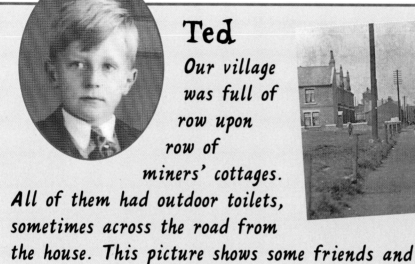

Ted

Our village was full of row upon row of miners' cottages. All of them had outdoor toilets, sometimes across the road from the house. This picture shows some friends and me outside our house.

In some parts of the south of England, new houses were being built and people enjoyed a higher standard of living.

Sally

In 1945 we moved to a house in Kent. It was a new house that had been built in the late thirties and had many modern features.
This picture shows me on the lawn in front of the house with my pet rabbit, 'Wiggles'.

HOUSEWORK

Houses in the forties took a lot more time to clean and take care of than they do now. Few houses had fitted carpets. Most had wooden or tiled floors that had to be swept every day, and sometimes washed or polished.

WASHING

Mondays were often washdays. Washing was done by hand and clothes were hung on a line to dry. If it was raining, they would be hung in front of the fire.

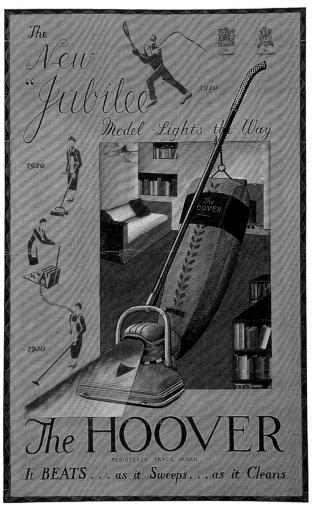

Roy

Washing was done in a shed in the back yard. Hot water came from the boiler in the back kitchen. Buckets were taken and emptied into the dolly tub together with the soap powder. The clothes were added and mixed around with the dolly legs. The clothes were then put through the mangle - if you were too slow your fingers got caught and it was very painful.

By the end of the decade, washing machines, vacuum cleaners and refrigerators were available to some housewives. They could spend less time doing housework.

13

RATIONING

During the war enemy warships and submarines sank hundreds of ships bringing food and supplies to Britain. This led to a serious shortage of food. Many foods were rationed so that everyone would get the same amount. Some of the first foods to be rationed were sugar, bacon, tea and butter. People had ration books which allowed them a certain amount of each food each week.

These are the rations for one person for a week.

Sally

This picture shows my sixth birthday party. The party was made possible because the Navy gave my mother some of their rations of sugar, flour and eggs. My mother was able to make biscuits, jellies and of course, a birthday cake. It was a great party.

Old Money

In the 1940s, British currency was made up of pounds, shillings and pence. There were twelve pence (12d) in a shilling (1/-), and twenty shillings (20/-) in a pound. As well as £20, £10 and £5 notes, there were also one pound notes and a ten shilling note.

THEN & NOW

- In 1948 a pint of milk cost 1d (less than $\frac{1}{2}$p), now it is 38p.

Clothing

There was very little material available for clothing during the war, and you needed clothing coupons to buy even a handkerchief. The government tried to encourage people to reuse old clothes and materials, and the phrase 'Make do and Mend' became very familiar. Housewives were very clever in the way they made children's clothes out of flour sacks, or unravelled jerseys to re-knit them into something else.

Towards the end of the forties, rationing was stopped on many items. There were still many shortages of some goods, and food rationing did not end completely until 1954.

SCHOOL

Schools in the 1940s were very different to today's schools. They were often located in cold and draughty buildings. The windows were high up so that the children could not look outside and be distracted from their lessons.

Each child had their own desk with a lid. The teacher had his or her own desk at the front of the class.

THEN & NOW

- Physical or corporal punishment was common in schools in the 1940s. Now it is illegal for a teacher to hit a child.

Ted

Our village had two schools, the infants, and the junior and senior combined. The classes were quite large and the teachers very strict. We were often punished for getting things wrong or being late for lessons.

LESSONS

Lessons were quite formal with an emphasis on learning things by heart. There were very few text books so most things had to be copied off the blackboard. Children wrote in exercise books with steel-nibbed pens and ink. Each child had an inkwell which fitted into their desk-top. It would be one child's duty to fill the ink wells each week.

During the war most of the male teachers had to leave their jobs to join the forces. Schools were usually left with an all-female staff.

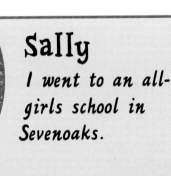

Sally

I went to an all-girls school in Sevenoaks.

There were only 15 children in my form. The picture shows a reading lesson in progress. We did not have many reading books, and sometimes had to share.

FREE MILK

Since the thirties the government paid for all children to have free school milk. This was to encourage the drinking of pasteurised milk, which was thought to be very healthy. The milk came in small bottles ($^1/_3$ pint, less than $^1/_4$ litre). Each child got their own bottle and a straw at mid-morning playtime.

Ted

My school had no central heating, just a huge stove in each classroom. The stove ran on coal that the caretaker carried around in large black coal scuttles. In winter, our daily milk allowance was warmed up in a saucepan on the stove. Sometimes, for a special treat, the teachers made us Horlicks!

Roy

My junior school was a four-storey Victorian building with a playground on the roof. We used to make parachutes out of pieces of paper and a stone, and throw them over the eight foot (2.5m) railings. The teachers were very cross if they caught you, because the infants' playground was in the yard below!

Diana

Like children today, I went to several classes outside school, like ballet, tap dancing and horse riding. This picture shows my sister and me on the way to our riding class. Everything was much more formal then, we had to wear jodhpurs, shirts and ties and of course, a riding hat.

SECONDARY SCHOOL

Before the war, most children left school at 14 to get a job. The 1944 Education Act said that all children had to stay at school until they were fifteen years old.

During the last year at junior school, each child had to take an exam called the 11 Plus. If they passed the 11 Plus they could go on to a grammar school or technical school. Children who did not pass the 11 Plus went to secondary modern schools.

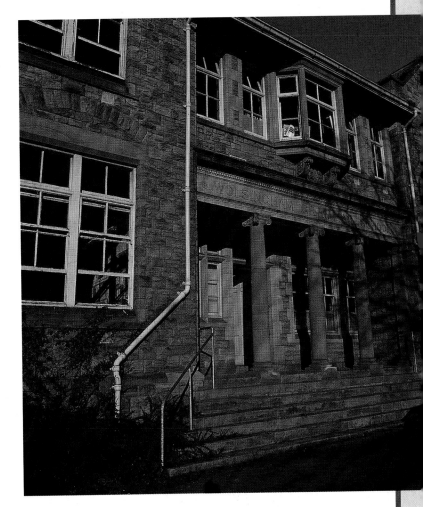

Wolsingham Grammar School.

Having Fun

Toys and Games

Children had very few toys in the forties. The war meant there was no money available either to manufacture or buy them. Toys were often made as miniature versions of the real things.

Sally

My favourite toys were my toy car and my dolls' pram. My car looked just like my grandfather's Wolseley and the pram was identical to my baby sister's!

• Lead soldiers were a popular toy in the forties. Now lead is known to be poisonous and is banned in toy production.

Most children had to make up their own games and find their own amusement. Many simple games such as skipping with a rope or playing hopscotch took place outside on the road. There were so few cars it was safe for children to play in the streets.

BOOKS AND COMICS

There were not many books available to children in the forties. Very few books were published during the war because there was little paper available. Most of the books children read were borrowed from libraries.

Diana

On Saturdays my sister and I went to visit my grandparents. They always bought us a comic each. Usually it was the Dandy and the Rainbow. We spent the rest of the day reading one comic and then swapped with each other to read the other one.

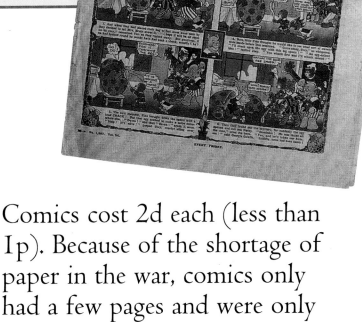

Comics cost 2d each (less than 1p). Because of the shortage of paper in the war, comics only had a few pages and were only printed every two weeks.

◀ The popular board game Monopoly was imported from America.

CINEMA

Cinemas in the forties were a much more important source of entertainment than they are now. They were very grand and were known as picture palaces. Films changed twice a week and many people would visit the cinema each time a new film was showing. As well as the

main film, there would be a supporting film called a 'B' Film and a newsreel of what was happening in the war.

Diana

To get into an 'A' film, you had to be accompanied by an adult. This was very annoying for me and my sister, as we could rarely persuade our parents to come to the cinema. We used to hang around the cinema entrance until we saw an adult going in and then ask if we could go in with them. I am sure parents would not let their children do this today.

THE WIRELESS

The wireless was a vital form of communication in the forties. For many people it was the main means of hearing about what was happening in the war. They would listen to the news regularly at 8 am, 1 pm and 9 pm. Every evening, 'Children's Hour' broadcast an hour of children's programmes between 5 and 6 pm.

TELEVISION

The BBC had started a television service in 1936. This was suspended during the war and did not start up again until 1946, when there were fewer than 12,000 viewers. Most households did not buy a television until the fifties.

PRICE SIXPENCE

"KEEP IT GOING!"

Roy

My dad built his own television set! With the help of a magazine called Practical Television, he converted an ex-War Department radar set into a television. It had a 6 inch (15 cm) green screen, so the picture wasn't great, but it seemed like magic then. This was in 1947 and we were the first people in the street to have a TV!

THEN & NOW

- Television started with black and white programmes and just one channel. Now there are five terrestrial channels and hundreds of satellite ones, and all programmes are in colour.

TRANSPORT

MOTORBIKES

There was very little petrol available in the forties. It was heavily rationed both during and after the war. Motorbikes were popular because they used less petrol than cars. Some motorbikes had side-cars for passengers to travel in. Helmets were not compulsory but many people wore caps and a pair of goggles.

BUSES

The countryside was well served by buses. All buses had a driver and a bus conductor. The bus conductor carried a ticket machine over his or her shoulder which issued the tickets.

Diana

We went everywhere on foot, by bike or by public transport. At weekends we travelled by bus. The bus tickets came in all different colours depending on the length of journey. My sister and I tried to collect a complete set and often asked other passengers for their used tickets.

CARS

Cars were much less comfortable than they are now. They had no heating, no radios and the seats were very cramped. Some cars had indicator lights on little stalks that popped out on either side of the car.

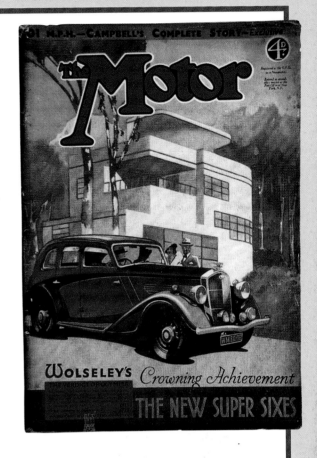

WOLSELEY'S *Crowning Achievement*
THE NEW SUPER SIXES

THEN & NOW

- A new car cost about £300 in the forties. A similar car now would cost about £12,000.

- A 6 km journey by bus cost 1d (about ½p) in the 1940s. Nowadays a similar journey would cost £2.50.

Sally

My grandfather had a Wolseley which was very smart and fun to travel about in. He bought it in 1937, and kept it until 1946 when it had to be sold because we could not afford to run it any more.

TRAINS

In the 1940s most trains were steam-driven although electric trains were starting to be used. During the war many trains and railway lines were damaged by bombs. It was hard to travel long distances.

All forms of public transport were very crowded during the war, because so many soldiers needed to travel about on them. People were asked not to make journeys unless they were really necessary.

IS YOUR JOURNEY REALLY NECESSARY?

RAILWAY EXECUTIVE COMMITTEE

In 1948 the railways were nationalized, and four separate companies merged into British Railways, which later became British Rail. Now there are separate companies again.

THEN & NOW

- In 1946 there were 32,000 km (20,000 miles) of railways. Today there are only 16,000 km (10,000 miles).

TRAMS

Trams were like buses but they were electric and ran on rails down the middle of the road. In the forties, most cities had a tram service and many people, especially children, found it an enjoyable way to travel.

Roy

Liverpool was home to many tramcars. There was one service, the No. 44, which ran for 12 miles to Kirkby. Liverpool City Public Transport ran a special price for city kids of one penny return for this journey. During the summer holidays the trams were full of kids with pennies, saying, 'Penny return to Kirkby Woods mister.' to the conductor. You had to look after your ticket carefully during the day otherwise it was a long walk home.

Trams were very much part of the road traffic and sometimes ran into cars or lorries.

AFTER THE WAR

VE Day

On 8 May, 1945 the war in Europe finally ended. This was known as VE Day. There were many celebrations. Street parties were held with balloons and flags and special food such as jelly and ice cream. Gradually the men and women in the armed forces began to return. Everyone was very happy, but most families had lost someone and many children were orphaned. Thousands of young women left Britain to marry American soldiers whom they had met during the war.

A VE Day street party

After the war the country was in a bad way. Many homes as well as factories, schools and docks had been smashed by bombs. Miles of roads and railways were worn out. The country owed millions of pounds of debts to other countries. There were still shortages of some types of food and fuel, and rationing continued for many years.

HOLIDAYS

During the war few people had holidays. Men were fighting abroad, there was little money available and many of the beaches were closed due to mines. With the end of the war, people started going on holiday again.

Diana

After the war we went on holiday to St Andrews in Scotland. We travelled up to Scotland on a sleeper train. This was very exciting except that my sister and I always quarrelled as to who was going to sleep on the top bunk! It was lovely to be able to play on the beach again.

Roy

Our holidays were always spent camping near the beach on the Wirral peninsula. We had fun playing in the water at high tide, and at low tide we collected cockles which we boiled up for supper.

ROYAL WEDDING

On 20 November 1947, Princess Elizabeth was married to Lieutenant Philip Mountbatten. The wedding took place in Westminster Abbey. Thousands of people lined the streets of London to watch the royal procession. Many more people listened to the event on the wireless. It was also filmed and shown in newsreels at cinemas all over the world.

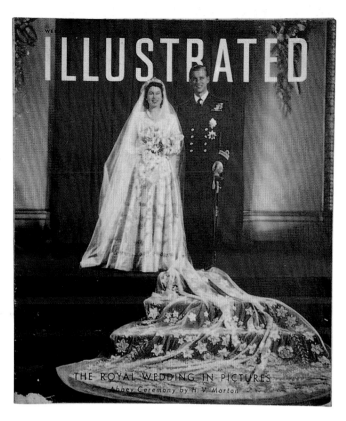

The royal wedding towards the end of the forties helped people realize that there were better times ahead, as they struggled with the difficult task of rebuilding their lives after the war.

May pole dancers celebrate May Day in a country village after the war.

FURTHER READING

History From Objects - *At School, In the Street, Keeping Clean* and *Toys,* Hodder Wayland

History From Photographs - *Clothes and Uniforms, Houses and Homes, Journeys, People Who Help Us, School, In the Home* and *In the Street,* Hodder Wayland

Take Ten Years - *1940s,* Ken Hills, Evans Brothers

Grandma's War, Rebecca Hunter, Evans Brothers 1999

Travelling in Grandma's Day, Faye Gardner, Evans Brothers 1997

Fiction:
War Boy, Michael Foreman, Pavilion

Carrie's War, Nina Bawden, Puffin

Goodnight Mister Tom, Michelle Magorian, Penguin

Back Home, Michelle Magorian, Puffin

GLOSSARY

air-raids: Bombing attacks from enemy aircraft.

Anderson shelters: Huts made of corrugated iron that people sheltered in during air raids.

corporal punishment: Punishment in school when children were smacked or beaten with a cane.

dolly tub: A wooden tub for doing the laundry in, before the days of washing machines.

Eleven (11) Plus: An exam children sat aged 11 to decide which school they would go on to.

evacuation: Moving children from the dangerous cities to the safer countryside during the war.

gas masks: Masks that were worn over the face to protect people from poisonous gases that might be used during the war.

Home Guard: An organization of men who were to help defend Britain from enemy invasion. They were originally called Local Defence Volunteers.

mangle: A machine with rollers for squeezing water out of wet laundry.

nationalized: Owned and run by the government.

ration book: A wartime book of coupons that was given to each person allowing them a certain amount of food each week.

Second World War: A war that involved many countries all over the world and lasted from 1939 until 1945.

shilling: An amount of money worth 12 old pence (5p).

VE Day: Victory in Europe Day. The day the war ended in Europe.

wireless: A radio set.

Women's Land Army: Women who left their homes to work on farms during the war.

INDEX